How to Analyze the Films of

THE COEN BROTHERS

by Susan E. Hamen

ABDO
Publishing Company

Essential Critiques

How to Analyze the Films of
THE COEN BROTHERS

by Susan E. Hamen

Content Consultant: Dr. Walter C. Metz, Professor and Chair
Department of Cinema and Photography, Southern Illinois University Carbondale

Credits

Published by ABDO Publishing Company, PO Box 398166, Minneapolis, MN 55439. Copyright © 2013 by Abdo Consulting Group, Inc. International copyrights reserved in all countries. No part of this book may be reproduced in any form without written permission from the publisher. The Essential Library™ is a trademark and logo of ABDO Publishing Company.

Printed in the United States of America,
North Mankato, Minnesota
042012
092012

 THIS BOOK CONTAINS AT LEAST 10% RECYCLED MATERIALS.

Editor: Mari Kesselring
Series Designer: Marie Tupy

Library of Congress Cataloging-in-Publication Data
Hamen, Susan E.
  How to analyze the films of the Coen brothers / Susan E. Hamen.
    p. cm. -- (Essential critiques)
  Includes bibliographical references.
  ISBN 978-1-61783-454-7
  1. Coen, Ethan--Criticism and interpretation--Juvenile literature. 2. Coen, Joel--Criticism and interpretation--Juvenile literature. 3. Film criticism--Juvenile literature. I. Title.
  PN1998.3.C6635H36 2012
  791.4302'330922--dc23
                                        2012005975

Table of Contents

1

Introduction to Critiques

What Is Critical Theory?

What do you usually do as a member of an audience watching a movie? You probably enjoy the settings, the costumes, and the sound track. You learn about the characters as they are developed through dialogue and other interactions. You might be drawn in by the plot of the movie, eager to find out what happens next. Yet these are only a few of many ways of understanding and appreciating a movie. What if you are interested in delving more deeply? You might want to learn more about the director and how his or her personal background is reflected in the film. Or you might want to examine what the film says about society—how it depicts the roles of women and minorities, for example. If so, you have entered the realm of critical theory.

Critical theory helps you learn how various works of art, literature, music, theater, film, and other endeavors either support or challenge the way society behaves. Critical theory is the evaluation and interpretation of a work using different philosophies, or schools of thought. Critical theory can be used to understand all types of cultural productions.

There are many different critical theories. If you are analyzing a movie, each theory asks you to look at the work from a different perspective. Some theories address social issues, while others focus on the director's life, what role the direction plays in the overall film, or the time period in which the film was written or set. For example, the

critical theory that asks how a director's life and
filmmaking style affected the work is called auteur
criticism. Other common, broad schools of criticism
include historical criticism, feminist criticism, and
ideological criticism.

What Is the Purpose of Critical Theory?

Critical theory can open your mind to new ways
of thinking. It can help you evaluate a movie from
a new perspective, directing your attention to issues
and messages you may not otherwise recognize in
a work. For example, applying feminist criticism to
a film may make you aware of female stereotypes
perpetuated in the work. Applying a critical theory
to a work helps you learn about the person who
created it or the society that enjoyed it. You can
explore how the movie is perceived by current
cultures.

How Do You Apply Critical Theory?

You conduct a critique when you use a critical
theory to examine and question a work. The theory
you choose is a lens through which you can view
the work, or a springboard for asking questions
about the work. Applying a critical theory helps you

to think critically about the work. You are free to question the work and make an assertion about it. If you choose to examine a film using auteur theory, for example, you want to know how the director's personal background, education, or filmmaking techniques inspired or shaped the work. You could explore why the director was drawn to the story. For instance, are there any parallels between a particular character's life and the director's life?

Forming a Thesis

Ask your question and find answers in the work or other related materials. Then you can create a thesis. The thesis is the key point in your critique. It is your argument about the work based on the tenets, or beliefs, of the theory you are using. For example, if you are using auteur theory to ask how the director's life inspired the work, your thesis could be worded as follows: Director Teng Xiong, raised in refugee camps in Southeast Asia, drew upon her experiences to direct the movie *No Home for Me.*

How to Make a Thesis Statement

In a critique, a thesis statement typically appears at the end of the introductory paragraph. It is usually only one sentence long and states the author's main idea.

Providing Evidence

Once you have formed a thesis, you must provide evidence to support it. Evidence might take the form of examples and quotations from the work itself—such as dialogue from a film. Articles about the movie or personal interviews with the director might also support your ideas. You may wish to address what other critics have written about the work. Quotes from these individuals may help support your claim. If you find any quotes or examples that contradict your thesis, you will need to create an argument against them.

For instance: <u>Many critics have pointed to the heroine of *No Home for Me* as a powerless victim of circumstances. However, through her dialogue and strong actions, she is clearly depicted as someone who seeks to shape her own future.</u>

How to Support a Thesis Statement

A critique should include several arguments. Arguments support a thesis claim. An argument is one or two sentences long and is supported by evidence from the work being discussed.

Organize the arguments into paragraphs. These paragraphs make up the body of the critique.

In This Book

In this book, you will read overviews of famous movies directed by the Coen brothers, each followed by a critique. Each critique will use one theory and apply it to one work. Critical thinking sections will give you a chance to consider other theses and questions about the work. Did you agree with the author's application of the theory? What other questions are raised by the thesis and its arguments? You can also find out what other critics think about each particular film. Then, in the You Critique It section in the final pages of this book, you will have an opportunity to create your own critique.

Look for the Guides

Throughout the chapters that analyze the works, thesis statements have been highlighted. The box next to the thesis helps explain what questions are being raised about the work. Supporting arguments have been underlined. The boxes next to the arguments help explain how these points support the thesis. Look for these guides throughout each critique.

Essential Critiques

Ethan, *left*, and Joel have worked together on
film projects since their youth.

2

A Closer Look
at the Coen Brothers

Brothers Joel and Ethan Coen were born and raised
in Saint Louis Park, a suburb of Minneapolis,
Minnesota. Joel, born November 29, 1954, and
Ethan, born September 21, 1957, have one older
sister, Deborah. The Coen children grew up in a
middle-class, Jewish, academic household. Their
father, Edward, was an economics professor at the
University of Minnesota, and their mother, Rena,
taught art history at Saint Cloud State, another
Minnesota university. Later, the Coen brothers
would base many of their films in the Midwest.

In an effort to combat boredom in the land of
long, cold Minnesota winters, the Coen brothers
immersed themselves in television and movies,
developing a particular interest in old films. In
their early teens, the Coen brothers pooled money

they had earned mowing lawns with neighbor Ron Neter and purchased a used Super-8 camera. Soon, the fledgling filmmakers were shooting their own movies. They shot remakes of films as well as a handful of originals, including one titled *Henry Kissinger—Man on the Go*.

Artistic Educations

Both Joel and Ethan have admitted to being underwhelmed with life in the Midwest. After attending a Hebrew high school, Joel convinced his parents to let him to transfer to a progressive high school called Simon's Rock in Great Barrington, Massachusetts. Students there were able to take college-level courses in conjunction with regular high school classes. In 1971, Joel moved to Massachusetts to attend the special school. When Ethan began high school in 1974, he followed in Joel's footsteps and attended Simon's Rock. The school turned out to be just the type of encouraging environment the brothers needed to nurture their artistic abilities.

Upon graduation in 1973, Joel attended New York University where he studied film. After earning his undergraduate degree, he worked as a production assistant on music videos and industrial films. His friend Sam Raimi, who would eventually become a highly successful film director and producer, provided Joel with the opportunity to work as assistant editor on his first feature film in 1981, *The Evil Dead*. Three years later, the Coens would be breaking into the film industry themselves.

Three years younger than Joel, Ethan graduated from Simon's Rock and entered Princeton University in 1977, where he majored in philosophy. After graduating in 1980, he moved to New York City to join Joel.

The Partnership Begins

Once reunited, the brothers began working on writing a screenplay. *Blood Simple*, the Coens' first stab at collaborating as writers and directors, was shot in 1982 and released two years later. The film received critical acclaim and was the first of what would be a long string of collaborative films. The Coens' notably eccentric, dark comedic, and violent style helped establish them as talented filmmakers. With *Blood Simple*, their film partnership was off to a successful start.

In 1987, *Raising Arizona*, their next major film, hit the big screen. Starring Nicolas Cage, Holly Hunter, and John Goodman, the film's plot follows an unlikely couple—an ex-convict and his wife, a former prison officer—and their plot to kidnap a baby from a wealthy couple with quintuplets. The offbeat comedy was a box office hit.

In the 1990s, many of the Coen brothers' films made it to the silver screen. Two well-received films were *Miller's Crossing* (1990), a mobster flick starring Gabriel Byrne and John Turturro, and *Barton Fink* (1991), a film that finds Turturro as a playwright struggling with writer's block in 1940s Hollywood. Their next film, *The Hudsucker Proxy* (1994), was not as successful.

Then, the brothers hit gold in 1996 with the dark comedy *Fargo*. Starring notable actors Frances McDormand, who had married Joel in 1984, William H. Macy, Steve Buscemi, and Peter Stormare, *Fargo* tells the tale of a man in serious financial trouble. The man's elaborate plot to get out of debt does not go as planned.

Fargo was met with critical acclaim and became a box office hit. In 1996, Joel received a Cannes Film Festival Award for Best Director.

The next year, the film was nominated for seven Academy Awards, bringing home Oscars for Best Original Screenplay for the brothers, as well as Best Actress for McDormand. Although both brothers shared the job of directing, the credits list Joel as the director and both brothers as writers. In 2006, the Library of Congress selected *Fargo* for preservation in the United States Film Registry.

Riding the wave of success following *Fargo*, the Coens' next project, *The Big Lebowski* (1998), did not prove to be an immediate smash hit. Still, the film further exemplified their artistic filmmaking talent.

Continuing with Success

In 2000, the Coens released *O Brother, Where Art Thou?*, which is a modern adaptation of Homer's epic poem *The Odyssey*. The film stars George Clooney, John Turturro, John Goodman, and Holly Hunter. The comedy, set during the Great Depression in the South, received favorable reviews and was nominated for two Academy Awards. *O Brother, Where Art Thou?* opened the Coens up to a wider audience. Many people were drawn in by the use of period-specific folk music, which earned the movie's sound track a Grammy for Album of the Year in 2001.

The duo continued to produce noteworthy films with big-name Hollywood stars: *The Man Who Wasn't There* (2001), *Intolerable Cruelty* (2003), and *The Ladykillers* (2004). The films found the Coen brothers working with Billy Bob Thornton, George Clooney and Catherine Zeta-Jones, and Tom Hanks, respectively.

The 2007 film *No Country for Old Men,* a film adaptation of Cormac McCarthy's novel of the same name, had the brothers once again collecting awards. Critics praised the dark crime thriller, and it received two Golden Globes and four Oscars.

Following their 2009 film, *A Serious Man*, the Coen brothers released a remake of a John Wayne classic, *True Grit*, in 2010. Avoiding their trademark dark comedy, the brothers sought to create a film faithful to Charles Portis's 1968 novel of the same name. The western, starring Jeff Bridges, Matt Damon, and newcomer Hailee Steinfeld, was a box office hit and earned an astounding ten Academy Award nominations.

Since 1984, the Coen brothers have worked on more than 20 film projects together. Actors often point out that the brothers work together seamlessly.

While fans are intimately familiar with the dark comedy, violence, and highly exaggerated performances characteristic of a Coen film, the brothers have also proven themselves to be successful in straightforward genres, such as the western. Many actors jump at the chance to work with the pair. The sibling collaborators continue to entertain audiences and surely have more award-winning screen writing and directing in their joint future.

Ethan, *left*, along with Joel, *right*, won Oscars for *No Country for Old Men* in 2008.

From left, Everett, Delmar, and Pete in a promotional image from O Brother, Where Art Thou?

3

An Overview of
O Brother, Where Art Thou?

O Brother, Where Art Thou? takes place in
Mississippi in 1937 during the Great Depression.
It opens with a chain gang swinging sledgehammers
and breaking rocks. Three prisoners, Ulysses
Everett McGill, Pete Hogwallop, and Delmar
O'Donnell, run across a field in a desperate effort to
escape Parchman Farm.

The men hitch a ride with an old blind man
pumping a manual railroad car. He prophesies their
future, saying he knows they seek a fortune. But the
man warns them, "First you must travel, a long and
difficult road, a road fraught with peril."[1]

The treasure the men seek is $1.2 million
Everett claims he stole from an armored car heist.
He says he buried the money before going to prison.
The men plan to make their way to Everett's family

farm to retrieve the money. However, they have only days before the area, the Arktabutla Valley, will be flooded to create a lake necessary for a new hydroelectric project.

The Journey Begins

Stopping at Pete's cousin Wash Hogwallop's farm, the men are freed of their chains. For the first time, the audience sees how particular Everett is about his hair, combing it thoroughly with Dapper Dan hair pomade and procuring a hairnet before turning in for the night.

Later that night, the men are awakened from their sleep in the barn, surrounded by the authorities. Wash has turned them in for the bounty. He explains, "Sorry, Pete. I know we're kin, but they got this depression on. I've got to do for me and mine."[2] As the officers set fire to the barn, Wash's young son rescues them, crashing a Ford Model T car through the barn. The men hop into the car, and the boy drives them away. The following day, the men send the boy walking back home and continue on their journey.

While resting in the woods along a river, a singing congregation makes its way to the riverbank for a mass baptism. Mesmerized and moved,

Delmar and Pete decide to be baptized. Everett chastises the two as fools for believing in baptism.

The three escapees record a hit song before continuing on their quest.

Journeying on, the three come to a crossroads, where they pick up a young African-American man named Tommy Johnson. Tommy claims he sold his soul to the devil in exchange for learning how to play the guitar. His description of Satan as a white man with empty eyes, a big hollow voice, and traveling with a hound coincidentally matches that of Sheriff Cooley. Cooley, along with his hound, continues to pursue the fugitives, led by the scent of Everett's pomade.

The four stop at a radio station owned by a blind man, where they make a quick buck recording the song "Man of Constant Sorrow." The song becomes an instant success on the airwaves, unbeknownst to the men on the run. On the way out, they run into Governor Pappy O'Daniel who is campaigning for a second term against the reform candidate, Homer Stokes.

After a brief encounter with George "Baby Face" Nelson, the men happen upon a group of women washing laundry by a river. The attractive women seduce them with singing and liquor. When Everett and Delmar come to, lying on the riverbank, Pete is nowhere to be found. His clothes are laid out on the ground and a toad hops out from them. Simpleminded Delmar believes the female sirens have transformed their friend.

The two travel on with the toad and run into Big Dan Teague, a one-eyed Bible salesman. Big Dan assaults both of them, steals their money, and squishes "Pete" the toad. The men press on, arriving in Everett's hometown. There, Everett learns his wife, Penny, has told their seven daughters he was hit by a train and killed. Penny is engaged to Vernon T. Waldrip, a man she claims has a job and is "bona fide."[3] The wedding is scheduled to take place the following day.

Pete's Return

After getting kicked out of the town's Woolworth store, Everett and Delmar visit the cinema. A group of prisoners enters, and Pete is among them. Pete warns them not to seek the treasure.

That night, Everett and Delmar break Pete out of jail. Pete explains the sirens turned him in for the bounty. He also admits that upon being whipped by authorities, he revealed the location of the treasure. But Everett explains he lied about the treasure all along. He decided to break out of prison to prevent Penny from remarrying. He came up with the treasure story to convince his chain mates to escape with him. This enrages Pete, who had only two weeks of his original sentence left, but he was given an additional 50 years for escaping.

Pete and Everett scuffle but are stopped by the sound of a Ku Klux Klan meeting. The trio sees the Klan has Tommy and plans to lynch him. Disguised as the mob's color guard, they intervene and save him. They discover gubernatorial candidate Homer Stokes is the great wizard of the Klan. Big Dan is also a Klansman. Everett cuts the support wires of a fiery cross, and it falls and crushes Big Dan to death.

Music and Politics

The men make it back to town where they sneak into a political fund-raiser dinner event for Homer disguised as musicians. As Delmar and Pete sing on stage, Everett once again tries to convince Penny to reconsider marrying Vernon.

When Homer shows up, he and Pappy get into a confrontation. But when the boys break into "Man of Constant Sorrow" up on stage, the whole place goes wild hearing the elusive Soggy Bottom Boys they have been hearing on the radio. For the first time, Everett and the other men see the popularity of their song. They are surprised by the crowd's response. Penny, too, is surprised to learn Everett is the man behind the hit record.

Homer interrupts their performance to excitedly tell the audience the men on stage interrupted a Klan meeting. The crowd runs Homer out of town on a rail, and Pappy sees his opportunity to utilize the Soggy Bottom Boys for his campaign. He grants Everett, Pete, and Delmar pardons. He plans to make them his brain trust for his second administration. The entire escapade having been broadcast on the radio, Pappy seems to have won back his constituency.

As they leave the fund-raiser, Penny and Everett are back together and plan to remarry the following day. However, Penny expects Everett to retrieve

Everett's goal throughout the film is to get home to his wife, Penny.

her wedding band, which is in the rolltop desk at the family farm. The family farm is located in the valley scheduled to be flooded the next day.

The Flood

When the trio, along with Tommy, arrives at the McGill home, they find Sheriff Cooley waiting for them. He is undeterred upon hearing they have been pardoned by the governor. He tells them to say their prayers before they are hanged. But just as Everett finishes asking God to help them, a large wall of water washes over the land and floods the entire valley.

As they struggle in the floodwaters, the rolltop desk floats up to them. Everett is able to retrieve the ring for Penny. Everett, Pete, Delmar, and Tommy survive the flood. As Pete and Delmar proclaim their safety a miracle, Everett reverts back to his stance that there is a perfectly scientific reason for the flood. He chastises the others for their faith. "That ain't the tune you was singin' back there at the gallows!"[4] Pete scolds him.

The ending scene of the movie shows Everett presenting Penny with the ring from the rolltop desk, only to have her inform him that the ring is not hers, but her Aunt Herlene's. As the McGill daughters sing as they walk behind their arguing parents, the blind African-American prophet can be seen pumping his way down the railroad track.

The theme of religion pervades the narrative of
O Brother, Where Art Thou?.

How to Apply New Criticism to *O Brother, Where Art Thou?*

What Is New Criticism?

New Criticism emerged as a style of literary analysis in the 1920s. New Criticism focuses on the work itself and disregards all other outside factors. New Criticism looks at a work's structure, diction, imagery, speech, and recurrent ideas and themes to determine how these elements come together to create a unified work.

Although New Criticism has classically been applied to books, stories, and poetry, New Criticism can be used to critique a film because a film is the product of a written screenplay. Film maintains the elements of the written story: dialogue, action, and setting.

Applying New Criticism to *O Brother, Where Art Thou?*

O Brother, Where Art Thou? is a quest as well as a religious journey toward salvation, on which the three convicts are put to the test both physically and spiritually. The trio travels from crushing rocks at a prison farm under the sweltering Mississippi sun—a metaphorical hell—to finding lifesaving salvation and pardon from both man and the Almighty. Throughout their journey, they repeatedly come into contact with themes of religion, sin, forgiveness, betrayal, and ultimately, redemption. But the movie serves more than just the purpose of portraying religious elements. *O Brother, Where Art Thou?* uses religious themes and representations throughout the film to reinforce the notions that morality equates salvation and that immorality leads to condemnation.

Throughout the film runs a continuous theme of salvation for those who live a moral life according to the teachings of Christianity. Everett's immorality

Thesis Statement

The thesis statement is stated at the end of the first paragraph: "*O Brother, Where Art Thou?* uses religious themes and representations throughout the film to reinforce the notions that morality equates salvation and that immorality leads to condemnation." This thesis addresses the question of how morality and immorality are represented in the film.

leads to a difficult life for him, and it is not until he repents for his sins that he is saved. Instead of endeavoring to make a living honestly through hard work, Everett works up one scheme after the next. Furthermore, he turns up his nose at religion, chastising Pete and Delmar for being baptized, telling them, "Baptism! You two are just dumber than a bag of hammers!"[1] It is also noteworthy to point out Everett's vanity regarding his hairstyle.

> **Argument One**
>
> The author begins to argue the thesis by describing Everett's immoral life, "Everett's immorality leads to a difficult life for him, and it is not until he repents for his sins that he is saved."

When the men face death, their faith is tested.

Pride is one of the seven deadly sins. Everett has a near addiction to Dapper Dan hair pomade. His need for the pomade ultimately allows the sheriff's hound to sniff out and track down the fugitives. It is not until the very end of the film, when faced with a hangman's noose, that Everett falls to his knees and begs God to save him so he can see his family again. At the very moment he acknowledges a higher power and repents of his sins, the three men and Tommy are saved and delivered from the hands of evil, depicted as Sheriff Cooley.

Argument Two

Here, the author points out the difference between true morality and feigned morality: "The film further promotes the idea that morality leads to salvation by presenting many characters who claim to be faithful but are not moral."

<u>The film further promotes the idea that morality leads to salvation by presenting many characters who claim to be faithful but are not moral.</u> Big Dan, for example, is a Bible salesman, putting the word of God in people's hands every day. However, he is a greedy brute. He admits to taking advantage of people "lookin' for answers" during "these times of woe and want," and he finally explains, "It's all about the money, boys!"[2] He then proceeds to beat Everett and Delmar half to death, and he steals their

money. We discover later that Big Dan is a member of the Ku Klux Klan. It is here where he meets his demise, taken down by a cross. Big Dan's immoral life of greed and violence leads him to his death.

The men are tempted by women bathing in the river, testing their baptismal pledge of morality.

Upon being baptized, Pete and Delmar choose to turn from lives of crime and elect to walk the straight and narrow henceforth. This plan lasts until they run into the sirens. <u>Pete's eventual immorality is quickly answered with condemnation.</u> Pete

Argument Three
The author addresses Pete's immorality: "Pete's eventual immorality is quickly answered with condemnation."

succumbs to the temptations of the sirens and is believed to be turned into a toad as a punishment for having sex out of wedlock. "Way I see it, he got what he deserved, fornicating with some whore of Babylon," Everett states.[3] "These things don't happen for no reason. . . . It's obviously some kinda judgment on his character."[4] Although they later discover Pete has not been turned into a toad, sex and liquor do land him back in prison, whipped, and nearly hanged. Promiscuity, or casual sex, is a common sin of immorality, and nearly causes Pete's demise.

Conclusion
In the final paragraph, the author reiterates her thesis and sums up her arguments that support it.

Rife with biblical parallels, from Wash betraying Pete to the authorities for money (Judas collecting his silver pieces for betraying Jesus) to an almighty flood washing away evil from the land (or in this case, the devilish lawman Sheriff Cooley), *O Brother, Where Art Thou?* is a demonstrative piece regarding the perils of sinful lives. The men who survive in the end are the ones who realize the error in their ways, repent, and ask for forgiveness.

Thinking Critically about *O Brother, Where Art Thou?*

Now it is your turn to assess the critique. Consider these questions:

1. The theme of baptism appears in the film literally as well as figuratively. In the end of the film, the dam breaks, and the deluge of water saves Everett, Pete, and Delmar from being hanged. What other religious themes appear in the work?

2. Do you think the author made a strong argument? What were the strongest points? What were the weakest points? Can you think of any evidence the author could have added to this argument?

3. What do you think about the concept of "every man for himself" that is suggested when Pete's cousin turns them in for the bounty? Which do you believe to be more immoral: Wash's betrayal or Pete's status of escaped convict? Explain.

Other Approaches

What you have just read is one possible way to apply New Criticism to *O Brother, Where Art Thou?* Following are two additional examples of how to apply this theory.

The Dialogue

The dialogue throughout the film is a quick-witted mix of Deep South twang and slang, humorously intertwined with educated ramblings. The thesis statement for such a critique could be: The dialogue in *O Brother, Where Art Thou?* creates an essential element of humor in a film about serious issues in the United States during the Great Depression.

The Father Figure

The concept of fatherhood is one point of focus throughout the movie. When Everett is rejoined with Penny, he argues that, although he has not done much for his girls, he is the paterfamilias and believes this to be a solid enough reason for her to take him back. Additionally, the concept of God as father to all mankind runs throughout the film. Everett represents the prodigal son, returning to the arms of God only when there is nowhere left to turn.

The thesis statement for this critique could be: Throughout *O Brother, Where Art Thou?*, the theme of father and child relationships is explored, specifically whether love and acceptance of each is something earned or something inherently given.

Jerry Lundegaard hatches a kidnapping plot to obtain money
he needs to get out of debt.

5

An Overview of
Fargo

Fargo takes place in Minnesota in 1987. The film opens with a man meeting two men at a bar in Fargo, North Dakota. He introduces himself as Jerry Lundegaard. The other men are Carl Showalter and Gaear Grimsrud. Jerry, a car salesman who is experiencing severe financial woes unbeknownst to his family, has made arrangements to hire the two criminals to kidnap his wife, Jean. He has agreed to give the men the brand new Oldsmobile Cutlass Ciera he has hauled with him, along with $40,000 cash, half of the planned $80,000 ransom he intends to get from his wealthy father-in-law, Wade Gustafson, who owns a car dealership and for whom Jerry works. However, Jerry's plans quickly unravel.

Financial Woes and Schemes

Back in Minneapolis, Minnesota, Jerry returns home to find his father-in-law there, and to his dismay, the man stays for supper. It is clear Wade tries to keep every member of his family under his thumb and has special contempt for Jerry.

Later, Wade calls Jerry to tell him he and his accountant Stan Grossman are interested in hearing more about a real-estate deal Jerry proposed to him. Buoyed up by the thought that he is close to getting his hands on $750,000, Jerry scrambles to call off the kidnapping, but Shep Proudfoot, the mechanic who put him in touch with Gaear, has no way of contacting the hit men.

Meanwhile, the car financing company is breathing down Jerry's neck to provide serial numbers for nonexistent cars that he took out a $320,000 loan against. He does his best to keep them at bay until he can get his hands on money from one of his impending schemes.

Wade and Stan tell Jerry they are pleased with the investment proposal and ask him what he expects for a finder's fee. Jerry counters that he is not looking for a finder's fee, that it is his deal, and he wants a loan of $750,000 to pursue it. Wade

refuses, telling Jerry he is not a bank. Knowing that a 10 percent finder's fee will not begin to cover his debt, Jerry becomes despondent.

Jerry hires villains Gaear, *left*, and Carl to kidnap Jean.

Kidnapping Leads to Murder

Carl and Gaear break into Jerry and Jean's home and kidnap Jean. They take her north to the Brainerd, Minnesota, area. On the way, they kill a state trooper who pulls them over and two teenage witnesses who drive past and see the grisly scene.

Seven-months-pregnant Marge Gunderson, Brainerd's chief of police, is awakened and summoned into work with the news of the triple homicide. Her husband, Norm, a wildlife painter, gets up with her in order to make her a breakfast of eggs before she leaves. The two seem homey and comfortable together.

Marge and another older, amiable officer named Lou inspect the scene of the crime. While Lou brings her coffee, Marge soon deduces the series of events. They get a lead from a hotel that registered the Ciera a few nights before and learn from the front desk clerk that the men had company. Marge talks to two prostitutes the men hired who report the suspects planned on heading to the Twin Cities.

It All Falls Apart

Meanwhile, Jerry meets with Wade and Stan. He nervously explains that Jean has been kidnapped and the kidnappers insist on dealing only with him. He claims they will kill Jean if the cops become involved. He also says the ransom is $1 million, instead of the $80,000 the kidnappers believe the ransom to be. Jerry intends to pocket the difference. As Jerry bungles his way through trying to gain control of the decision making, Wade insists they involve the police. Finally, Stan convinces Wade they should not take any chances with Jean's life. They agree to await further instructions from the kidnappers.

Carl and Gaear take Jean to a cabin on Moose Lake near Brainerd. After several days, Carl succumbs to boredom and begins losing his patience. He phones Jerry and tells him of the Brainerd murders and that they now want the entire $80,000 ransom. Frustrated and on edge, Jerry struggles to keep it together.

Marge drives down to Minneapolis to investigate some phone calls made from the hotel lobby pay phone where the suspects stayed. She questions Shep at the dealership. She then stops in Jerry's office to ask if a Ciera was stolen off the lot. Although he tells her no, he is clearly rattled by her questioning.

That night, Carl calls Jerry and tells him to meet him in 30 minutes at a parking ramp. However, Jerry's father-in-law insists on going instead. When Wade arrives with a case of money, Carl demands to know where Jerry is. Angered when Wade refuses to give him the money without Jean in exchange, Carl shoots Wade. When Carl reaches for the case of money, Wade shoots him, badly grazing the side of his face. Carl retaliates by killing Wade.

Returning to the Brainerd area, Carl stops on the road and finds $1 million in the briefcase instead of $80,000. Shocked, he takes out $80,000 and buries the rest in the snow along a fence line, seemingly to return later to procure it all for himself.

The next day in Minneapolis, Marge again inquires with Jerry about the stolen Ciera. He becomes belligerent, not wanting to answer her questions. "Sir, you have no call to get snippy with me," she tells him.[1] Huffily, he tells her he will do a lot count immediately, so he puts on his coat and stomps outside. Waiting in his office, Marge sees Jerry pull out of the dealership, fleeing the interview.

Meanwhile, Carl returns to the cabin and finds Gaear eating in front of the television and Jean dead on the floor. Carl gives Gaear his half of the $80,000 and the keys to his truck. He plans on taking the Ciera. However, Gaear insists on being compensated for half of the car's value. Enraged, Carl points out that he was the one who retrieved the money and was shot in the face doing so. As Carl leaves the cabin, Gaear follows him, attacking and killing him with an axe.

Before returning to the police station, Marge takes a drive around Moose Lake and spots the missing Ciera. She stops to investigate and comes upon Gaear feeding human limbs into a wood chipper. When he sees her, he takes off running across the frozen lake. Marge apprehends him by shooting him in the back of the leg.

Later, at a motel outside of Bismarck, North Dakota, the authorities apprehend Jerry. The movie ends with Marge and Norm watching television in bed, snuggling and chatting as if nothing has happened. The remaining $920,000 presumably remains buried.

Unlike Jerry and Lou, Marge is dominant and takes charge
of the crime in her city.

How to Apply Gender Criticism to *Fargo*

What Is Gender Criticism?

Gender criticism explores how an artistic work conveys ideas about men and women. While feminist criticism generally looks at the portrayal of women, gender criticism seeks to understand how the creative piece depicts what is masculine and what is feminine. Gender criticism considers how each gender is portrayed by the characters, how they interact, and how they are perceived. Gender criticism broadly analyzes the work to consider how the piece's depiction of what is masculine and feminine reflects society's notion of gender.

Applying Gender Criticism to *Fargo*

Throughout film and literature history, men have typically been showcased as the strong, able leaders, saving damsels in distress, solving the crimes, and saving the day. Women, on the other hand, are generally cast in the light of needing to be rescued, looking to men for protection and answers, and oftentimes being nothing more than the hero's love interest. However, in *Fargo*, these gender stereotypes are challenged. Fargo subverts some of the stereotypical assumptions about gender by presenting female characters who are rational and powerful and male characters who seem unfit to hold leadership roles.

The biggest deviation from the typical gender stereotypes in *Fargo* is Marge. The Coens reverse the gender disparity by empowering Marge as the movie's heroine without giving her extraordinary physical skills or great beauty. Marge has a keen intuition where the murder case is concerned. Although she is by no means forceful or brazen, always keeping her manners and demeanor

---

Thesis Statement

The thesis statement is stated at the end of the paragraph: "*Fargo* subverts some of the stereotypical assumptions about gender by presenting female characters who are rational and powerful and male characters who seem unfit to hold leadership roles." The thesis answers questions about how gender is portrayed in the film.

Argument One

The author begins to argue the thesis with this statement: "The Coens reverse the gender disparity by empowering Marge as the movie's heroine without giving her extraordinary physical skills or great beauty." This argument shows how Marge subverts traditional female stereotypes.

about her, she proves to have a good head on her shoulders. Throughout the film, Marge is never shown answering to anyone, man or woman. And even though she is a female in a dangerous line of work and pregnant, her husband and coworkers never treat her as though she needs to be protected. At the end of the film, Marge takes down Gaear single-handedly with little struggle. The Coens forfeit using the common scene of a male partner rushing in at the end to help the female apprehend the perpetrator. Not once does Marge need a man to rescue her. This is in direct contrast to how gender roles have historically been displayed in film and literature.

Deviating from the typical male cop stereotypes, Marge's partner, Lou, is portrayed as less intelligent than Marge in his crime-solving abilities. When the audience first meets Lou, he is seen performing traditionally female duties. He fetches and holds Marge's coffee for her while she inspects the scene of the crime and the bodies of the victims. On the drive back into town, Marge asks

> **Argument Two**
>
> Here, the author provides another example of how the film portrays gender: "Deviating from the typical male cop stereotypes, Marge's partner, Lou, is portrayed as less intelligent than Marge in his crime-solving abilities." The author is now focusing on how men are represented in the film.

Lou if he has looked in the murdered state trooper's citation book for the last entry. Lou reports the last vehicle entered had license plates reading "DLR." Lou then puts out an all-points bulletin for a car matching the description with license plates starting with "DLR." Trying to gently point out his mistake, Marge offers, "I'm not sure that I agree with you 100 percent on your police work there, Lou. . . . I think that vehicle there had dealer plates."[1] Lou's detective work is far inferior to Marge's.

> **Argument Three**
> The author addresses the point that the male protagonist in this film is neither smart nor capable: "Jerry, the male protagonist, is often seen as a blundering character that has little to no control at home, at work, or even over the kidnapping scheme he has devised."

Jerry, the male protagonist, is often seen as a blundering character that has little to no control at home, at work, or even over the kidnapping scheme he has devised. The first glimpse the audience gets of Jerry is his meeting with Carl and Gaear. Immediately, Carl puts him to task for being late, which Jerry reciprocates with his clumsy explanations. He is a man easy to insult and easier still to control. This is far from the typical gender stereotype that paints men as heroes who take charge of difficult or dangerous situations.

Jerry is not the master of his own domain either. This is clear when Wade, who is both his father-in-law and boss, comes for supper. When Jerry makes an attempt at small talk, Wade dismisses him. As supper comes to an end, Jerry and Jean's son Scotty asks to be excused so he can meet friends at McDonald's. Before his parents even have a chance to respond, Wade announces his disapproval, clearly disregarding Jerry's parental role. Jerry makes no attempt whatsoever to admonish his father-in-law for overstepping boundaries. He just accepts the situation.

Many of the men in *Fargo*, including Jerry, do not perform traditional male roles.

Later, when Jerry discusses the ransom plan with Wade and Stan, it is not until another man, Wade's accountant, agrees with Jerry, pointing out that Jean's life is at stake, that Wade begins to agree to the plan. Jerry simply supports the accountant's point with, "You're darn tootin'!"[2] Even when Jerry makes an attempt at being bold and assertive, he comes off more comical and cartoonish than serious. Jerry lacks the masculinity and power that accompany a stereotypical protagonist.

Conclusion

The final paragraph concludes the author's critique and sums up the arguments that support the assertion of the thesis.

Throughout the Coens' *Fargo*, Marge retains the traditional gender roles of a loving wife and nurturing mother-to-be, while also being portrayed as more rational and powerful than her male counterparts. Conversely, the male characters of Jerry and Lou, the male head of the household and the male cop, are seen as lacking power and confidence and struggling with their lack of problem-solving abilities. Between these three characters, the Coens prove ability is not gender specific while overturning classic notions of what constitutes masculinity and femininity.

Thinking Critically about *Fargo*

Now it is your turn to assess the critique. Consider these questions:

1. The thesis statement proclaims the film subverts stereotypical assumptions about gender. Do you agree with this? Why or why not?

2. What additional arguments could the author have made that stem from the plot, characters, or additional elements that would have helped to support the thesis?

3. In what other ways could gender criticism be applied to this film?

Other Approaches

You have just read one way to apply gender criticism to *Fargo*. Following are two additional approaches.

Fargo as Reinforcing Gender Roles

Although Marge is an astute officer and succeeds in the end, she is the only female in the movie portrayed as the equal to a man. The other female characters, including Jean and the two prostitutes the kidnappers hire, all represent age-old female roles: wife, mother, and prostitute. With these characters, one could argue the filmmakers reinforce the stereotypes of gender roles.

A thesis statement that focuses on how Jean supports gender stereotypes might be: Jean's life of domestic submission reaffirms stereotypical gender norms and supports the theory that a wife's place is at home.

Flexible Gender Roles among Characters

When we discuss gender roles, we typically think of the characteristics of masculinity and femininity in relation to men and women. Gender roles are socially constructed and are defined by social norms. However, gender roles can develop and flow between two people regardless of the type of relationship or what biological gender they might be. If you apply the typical masculine and feminine traits to Jerry and Wade, one is dominant while the other battles for equality. In the context of that relationship, Jerry takes on the feminine gender role.

The thesis statement for such a critique could be: *Fargo* explores the idea that gender roles are not inherently male or female and bends the stereotypes to transcend to all manner of human relationships.

From left, the Dude, Walter, and Donny spend most of their time at the bowling alley before the Dude is mistaken for the Big Lebowski.

7

An Overview of
The Big Lebowski

The Big Lebowski opens with a narrator, called "the Stranger," explaining that the story is about a man, Jeffrey Lebowski, who refers to himself as "the Dude," and takes place in the early 1990s.

As the Dude is returning from the grocery store to his apartment in the Venice neighborhood of Los Angeles, California, two men who are waiting for him accost him. The thugs demand money, one of them stating, "Your wife owes money to Jackie Treehorn," while the other urinates on the Dude's rug.[1] However, they eventually realize they are roughing up the wrong Jeffrey Lebowski and leave.

Later, the Dude is bowling with his friends Walter Sobchak, a Vietnam War veteran who is still obsessed with the war, and Donny Kerabatsos, a sweet-tempered simpleton who is constantly a latecomer to conversations. The Dude comes to the conclusion that he should pursue compensation for his ruined rug from the millionaire Jeffrey Lebowski, the one whom the thugs were after.

The next day, he meets with the wheelchair-bound millionaire, the Big Lebowski, at his mansion in Pasadena. The Big Lebowski refuses to compensate the Dude for his rug. The millionaire berates him for being a bum and dismisses him. On his way out, the Dude meets the Big Lebowski's young trophy wife, Bunny, lounging by the pool. The Dude then departs, taking with him a rug from the mansion.

A Kidnapping

The following day, the Dude is summoned back to the Lebowski mansion where the Big Lebowski informs him that Bunny has been kidnapped and held for a ransom of $1 million. He offers to pay the Dude $20,000 to act as courier, delivering the ransom money. The Dude agrees, speculating that Bunny has kidnapped herself in order to get her hands on the ransom money. The Big Lebowski gives him a pager so he can contact him as soon as the ransom and location are finalized.

Back at his apartment, the Dude is again assaulted and knocked out by a new set of thugs who steal the rug he took from the Big Lebowski mansion. The Dude awakens to the sound of the pager going off.

At the mansion, the Big Lebowski's assistant, Brandt, gives the Dude a silver briefcase and a portable phone and tells him to drive north and await the kidnappers' phone call for further instructions. However, the Dude picks up Walter who has brought a "ringer" case filled with his dirty underwear, insisting they keep the $1 million. However, the two mess up the money drop-off and are left with the suitcase containing the money, but no Bunny. Walter shakes off their failure and suggests they go bowling. While at the bowling alley, the Dude's car—along with the money—is stolen.

Maude Lebowski, the woman who stole the Dude's new rug, phones and asks the Dude to meet her at her studio. She is the Big Lebowski's grown daughter. She informs the Dude that Bunny is a pornography starlet who has been having an affair with Jackie Treehorn, a famous porn producer.

Maude tells him she and her father are both trustees for the Lebowski Foundation, but that her father's withdrawal of the $1 million ransom from the foundation constitutes embezzlement. Maude, too, believes the kidnapping to be a hoax. She asks the Dude to recover the ransom money. If the Dude helps her, she will reward him with $100,000.

When Maude's driver drops the Dude at home, the Big Lebowski and Brandt are waiting for him in a limo. They demand answers. After much stammering, the Dude states that he believes Bunny has kidnapped herself. In response, Brandt gives him an envelope containing a toe, presumably Bunny's.

After being threatened at home by three German nihilists who claim to be the kidnappers and who demand to know where the ransom is, the Dude picks up his car at the impound lot. The briefcase of money is missing from the car. Later, Maude tells the Dude that the leader of the nihilists, Uli, is a friend of Bunny's.

Jackie Treehorn's thugs return that evening and take the Dude to Jackie's beach house, where Treehorn offers the Dude a 10 percent finder's fee if he retrieves the money Bunny owes him. He drugs the White Russian he mixes for the Dude, leading the Dude to pass out.

Revealing the Scheme

When the Dude returns home, his apartment has been ransacked. However, Maude is also there and tells the Dude to have sex with her. Afterward, Maude admits that she hopes to conceive a child, but she explains she does not want the father to have any part in raising the child. She also tells him the family wealth is from her late mother's side, left entirely to the family charity. She further explains that her father has no money and lives off an allowance she provides. Upon hearing this, the Dude instantly unravels the

Maude convinces the Dude to help with her plot.

entire scheme and calls Walter and asks him to
come pick him up and to take him to Pasadena.

Meanwhile, the German nihilists order pancakes
at a restaurant. With them is the girlfriend of one
of the members, whose foot is bandaged, a toe
missing.

In Walter's van, the Dude reveals the whole
scheme to his friend. The Big Lebowski took
advantage of his wife's apparent kidnapping as
a way of getting rid of her. He hired the Dude,
knowing the man was a loser and would surely
botch the handoff. "The million bucks was never in
the briefcase," the Dude says. "[He] was hoping that
they would kill her," he points out.[2] The nihilists,
Bunny's friends, also seized the opportunity to
stage a fake kidnapping as a way to get money from
Bunny's wealthy husband.

They reach the Lebowski mansion and find
Bunny has returned from an impromptu trip
to Palm Springs, a trip that she did not tell her
husband about. Walter and the Dude confront the
Big Lebowski. They accuse him of using Bunny's
alleged kidnapping as an excuse to get money and
then pinning it on the Dude. The Big Lebowski does
not deny it.

One More Fight

Later, believing the affair to be behind them, the Dude and his friends go bowling. When the trio leaves the bowling alley, they find the Dude's car has been set ablaze by the three German nihilists who then demand the ransom money. Walter and the Dude explain that they know everything and that there is no ransom money. Uli demands the money in the men's wallets instead, which enrages Walter. He defends himself and his friends against the nihilists, beating them up. Donny, however, has a heart attack and dies.

Days later, the Dude and Walter pick up Donny's ashes, opting to take him away in a Folger's coffee can instead of paying $180 for an urn. They release his ashes on a cliff overlooking the ocean. Walter then suggests they go bowling.

At the bowling alley, the Dude runs into the Stranger who was the narrator at the opening of the film. He tells the Dude to take it easy, to which the Dude replies with his final words of the movie, "Well, you know. The Dude abides."[3] The Stranger says he knows there is a little Lebowski on the way, confirming Maude did in fact conceive from her tryst with the Dude.

The Dude has a laidback attitude toward life.

How to Apply Archetypal Criticism to *The Big Lebowski*

What Is Archetypal Criticism?

Archetypal criticism evaluates a book, film, or other piece of art through a main character or a central idea with which most people can identify, called an archetype. An archetype is a commonly recurring symbol in real life or in literature and is easily recognizable by most people. A reader or a viewer can readily relate to these common symbolic individuals or themes. Carl Jung first made famous the idea of the collective unconscious that is shared among people that causes them to recognize a similar cast of characters and situations. Joseph Campbell later expanded Jung's ideas recognizing similar narrative patterns in literary works around the world.

Some of the more familiar archetypal characters are the hero, the trickster, the seductress, the warrior, the nonconformist, the underdog, and the mother or father figure. The list of archetypes is wide ranging and also includes such common characters as the martyr, the devil, the wise old sage or magician, the goddess, and the Christ figure. But archetypes are not limited to people, and they can include ideas or concepts. Common nonliving archetypes are birth, death, rebirth, the quest, forbidden fruit, harvest, seasons, fear, or loss. The reader or the viewer connects with these people or ideas and shares emotionally in their experiences.

Applying Archetypal Theory to *The Big Lebowski*

The Coen brothers' 1998 cult classic hit *The Big Lebowski* is a film that, on the surface, is about mistaken identity, greed, and bowling. Although the movie takes place in 1991, the bulk of the movie's characters seem to fit better in the 1970s. The Dude, half slacker and half hippie, passes his time by drinking White Russians, bowling, smoking weed, and in general being very "Dude-like." Walter, his best friend, still wears his dog tags from Vietnam, is quick to lose his temper, and considers pacifism an emotional problem. Add to this scene swanky parties at a pornographer's beach house and polyester bowling uniforms, and the stage is set for a film rife with symbolic themes. The characters in *The Big Lebowski* are presented as established archetypes, but they challenge the common characteristics of these archetypes.

The film's protagonist, the Dude, is shown as the common archetype of the trickster, a character who disobeys conventional behavior, but he later transcends this archetype for that of the hero. The trickster character appears in many cultures. In the United States, the trickster is most common in Native-American literature. The trickster often plays tricks on other characters and is usually a "bad guy" character. The trickster lives on the edge of society, as does the Dude. The Coens introduce the Dude at the beginning of the film as a person who has no qualms about visiting the grocery store in a T-shirt, shorts, bathrobe, and

---

Thesis Statement

Here, the author states her thesis: "The characters in *The Big Lebowski* are presented as established archetypes, but they challenge the common characteristics of these archetypes." The thesis answers questions about how the characters in the film differ from traditional archetypes.

Argument One

The author makes her first argument defending her thesis statement: "The film's protagonist, the Dude, is shown as the common archetype of the trickster, a character who disobeys conventional behavior, but he later transcends this archetype for that of the hero." The author shows how the Dude's archetype changes in the film.

sunglasses even though it is nighttime. The Dude's wardrobe and shaggy, unkempt beard and hair suggest he cares very little about his appearance. In this way, he is rebelling against social norms. He does not have a job, and his recreational activities include bowling, driving around, and experiencing the occasional acid flashback.

The Dude advises people to "Just take it easy, man" and does not get worked up very easily.[1] In fact, when Treehorn's thugs jump him in the beginning of the film, he is quick to respond to their violence with biting humor rather than fear. As the blond thug repeatedly pushes his head into the toilet, demanding to know where the money is, the Dude offers, "Uh, it's uh– Oh– Uh– It's down there somewhere. Let me take another look."[2] After the other thug calls him a loser and urinates on the rug, the Dude responds, "Well, at least I'm housebroken."[3]

In William J. Hynes's essay on the characteristics of mythical tricksters, he states, "The trickster seems impelled inwardly to violate all taboos, especially those which are sexual, gastronomic, or scatological."[4] The Dude fits this part of the archetype as well. When Maude asks the

Dude to have sex with her, he immediately obliges. Later, he is unfazed when he finds out her ulterior motive of becoming pregnant by him. Furthermore, at the Lebowski mansion, the Dude stops to flirt with Bunny, not caring that he is doing it in front of her husband's loyal assistant.

However, while the Dude rambles his way through trials as the movie progresses, he transforms from the trickster to the hero. He trades in his low-key attitude when he receives the toe he believes to be Bunny's. He begins to worry that the situation is not as simple as he once thought. He finds a moral drive and is the one to discover the complex scheming that is taking place.

Brave and intelligent, Walter first seems to perform the father archetype, but his unsteady moral compass is atypical to this archetype. While Walter is arrogant and easily loses his cool, he is quickly turned around by his strict adherence to his moral code. As the father, Walter tries to set down the rules. When yelling at the Dude, he interrupts himself to point out, "Also, Dude,

> **Argument Two**
> The character of Walter and his archetype are explored: "Brave and intelligent, Walter first seems to perform the father archetype, but his unsteady moral compass is atypical to this archetype."

Chinaman is not the preferred nomenclature. Asian-American, please."[5] However, Walter's immorality challenges the archetype he performs. He shows little concern for Bunny and assures the Dude there is nothing to worry about. At the bowling alley, though, Walter loses his cool when he accuses another bowler of stepping over the foul line. Walter informs him, "Smokey, this is not 'Nam. This is bowling. There are rules."[6] The two argue about whether Smokey truly stepped over the line, and Walter pulls a gun on the man, shouting, "Has the whole world gone crazy? Am I the only one around here who [cares] about the rules?"[7] Walter calms down when Smokey marks his score as zero. "It's a league game, Smokey," he calmly explains, regaining his composure.[8] A kidnapped young woman who supposedly is on the brink of getting killed does not warrant much worry from Walter, but stepping over the foul line in bowling calls for weapons to be drawn.

Maude, the overtly feminist artist, seems to symbolize the bad girl archetype, but Maude subverts the archetype

Argument Three
The author begins her argument about Maude: "Maude, the overtly feminist artist, seems to symbolize the bad girl archetype, but Maude subverts the archetype by being selfless in unexpected ways."

by being selfless in unexpected ways. Maude admits when she meets the Dude that her father does not approve of her lifestyle. She is sexually promiscuous, creates her artwork in the nude, and her preferences in style, fashion, music, and friends are not mainstream. Yet she does not care how she is perceived or what people think of her. However, again, the Coens do not portray her as the typical bad girl. Although she lives a life of self-gratification, her motives are pure. Maude's reason for endeavoring to regain the money is to return it to the charity to which it truly belongs. In this way, Maude subverts her bad girl archetype.

Walter performs the father archetype but with no moral compass.

Conclusion

In the final paragraph, the author sums up how the Coens play with archetypes within *The Big Lebowski.*

With *The Big Lebowski*, the Coen brothers take a collection of commonly used tropes, stereotypes, and archetypes and play with them. The Dude is both the trickster and the hero. Walter is the father, but without the constant composure or morality. Maude is at once the bad girl and the seductress, yet she has the heart of a good girl. The result is a collection of eclectic characters that cannot neatly fall into the categories shared by the collective conscious.

Thinking Critically about *The Big Lebowski*

Now it is your turn to assess the critique. Consider these questions:

1. The first argument identifies the Dude as a trickster. Do you agree with this? Can you think of any arguments to refute this? What other archetype might he be?

2. What was the most interesting argument made? What other plot or character elements could be used to support this thesis?

3. Other archetypes exist in *The Big Lebowski*. What archetypes do you think Bunny, the Stranger, and the Big Lebowski are? What evidence from the film would you use to support these archetypes?

Other Approaches

The critique you have just read is one way to approach *The Big Lebowski* through the lens of archetypal criticism. The following are other ways to apply this approach.

The Quest

When we consider movies that deal with quests, films such as *The Lord of the Rings* or *Pirates of the Caribbean* may come to mind. The hero departs on an epic journey. He or she is tested, experiences loss, and must muster all the courage and strength he or she has to overcome evil in the end.

While not a typical tale of a hero striking out on a quest, there are undertones of the quest archetype throughout *The Big Lebowski*. The Dude is charged with the task of ultimately rescuing the young woman. When the plan goes awry, it would seem he has failed. But he is being tested. By the end of the movie, the Dude has come through his journey and emerged triumphant by being the one to uncover the many schemes afoot and by confronting the Big Lebowski.

A possible thesis for this argument might be: *The Big Lebowski* modernizes the archetypal idea of the quest to bring the protagonist through his journey with humor and satire rather than action and chivalry.

Stepmother and Stepchild

A perennial trope throughout legends has been the wicked stepmother. Evil, selfish, and greedy, this hostile female archetype has appeared in stories for centuries. Typically driven by economic motives, she has little love for her stepchildren and is often intent on getting them out of the picture (as is the case in *Hansel and Gretel* and *Snow White*).

With Maude and Bunny, *The Big Lebowski* re-explores the stepmother and stepchild relationship. Not only is Maude older and more mature, she is not dependent upon her stepmother at all. In fact, Maude provides an allowance to her father, who then gives Bunny an allowance. Therefore, in this case, the stepmother's financial security comes from the stepchild.

A possible thesis for this argument might be: *The Big Lebowski* subverts the historical wicked stepmother archetype by portraying Maude and Bunny in nontraditional roles of stepmother and stepchild through a shift in power.

In *True Grit*, young Mattie Ross goes in search of her father's murderer.

An Overview of
True Grit

True Grit opens with a voiceover of older Mattie Ross explaining that when she was 14, her father was gunned down by hired hand Tom Chaney in Fort Smith, Arkansas, after a night of drinking and card playing went awry. Chaney then stole her father's horse and two California gold pieces he always carried with him and fled. Yet, as Mattie explains, "He could have walked his horse, for not a soul in that city could be bothered to give chase."[1]

In the next scene, 14-year-old Mattie arrives in Fort Smith where she seeks out the local sheriff to inquire about the search for her father's killer. Upon hearing that Chaney has fled into Indian Territory, where the sheriff has no authority, she decides to hire a US marshal to pursue Chaney. When she asks the sheriff who the best marshal is, she is told, "Meanest is Rooster Cogburn. He is a pitiless man, double tough, and fear don't enter into his thinking."[2] She decides to seek out Cogburn, believing him to be a man who has "true grit."[3]

Reuben "Rooster" Cogburn, a surly, one-eyed man with little patience and a disinclination for conversation, coupled with a fondness for drinking, brushes her off as a child. Mattie next meets a Texas Ranger named LaBoeuf who is also in pursuit of Chaney. He intends to catch and return Chaney to Texas for a reward. He proposes he and Cogburn pursue the man together. Mattie refuses.

Mattie finds a sleeping Cogburn in the back room of a Chinese grocery. She finally convinces him to take the job, but he doubles the bounty to $100 because Chaney has fallen in with a ruthless band of outlaws led by Lucky Ned Pepper. Mattie agrees and plans to meet Cogburn at the Chinese grocery the following morning so they can head out to find Chaney together. However, when Mattie returns, she is given a train ticket and a note from Cogburn, instructing her to return home. Refusing to be left behind, Mattie rides after Cogburn and finds him riding with LaBoeuf. Cogburn allows her to join them, much to LaBoeuf's dismay.

Mattie learns that Cogburn and LaBoeuf have agreed to pursue Chaney together, return him to Texas, and split the reward money, which angers her. Mattie wants to be able to see Chaney brought to justice, which she cannot do if he's taken to Texas. But, after an argument between LaBoeuf and Cogburn, Cogburn decides to cancel their agreement. The men go their separate ways, and Mattie stays with Cogburn. "Congratulations, Cogburn," scoffs LaBoeuf. "You've graduated from marauder to wet nurse."[4]

Mattie teams up with Cogburn, *right*, and LaBoeuf, *middle*.

Outlaws

Later that night, LaBoeuf rides up to a dug-out shack, and Pepper and three members of his gang follow behind him. Cogburn and Mattie, hiding in the hills above the shack, look on as LaBoeuf is lassoed and dragged behind one of the outlaws' horses. Cogburn fires upon the outlaws, killing two of them. Yet Pepper escapes. LaBoeuf again joins Mattie and Cogburn.

The following night, around the campfire, a drunken Cogburn rebukes LaBoeuf, insisting that he should not eat since he was injured and not pulling his weight. Furthermore, Cogburn declares he washes his hands of the whole mission, stating, "I'm a foolish old man who has been drawn into a wild-goose chase by a harpy in trousers and a nincompoop!"[5]

LaBoeuf decides to leave that night, refusing to allow Mattie to join him. The two agree they misjudged the other and exchange their mutual respects. LaBoeuf rides away, leaving behind a saddened Mattie.

In the morning, Mattie runs into Chaney down at the river. He recognizes her, and she draws her father's pistol on him in an attempt to arrest him. Chaney laughs at her and approaches her. Mattie fires and hits him in the side. As he makes his way toward her, her pistol misfires, allowing Chaney the chance to seize her. He hauls her back to Pepper and the rest of the crew as Cogburn runs down to the river and fires at them. Pepper threatens to kill the girl unless Cogburn rides away.

Pepper leaves Mattie with Chaney, promising to send a man back later with a horse for him. He succinctly informs Chaney that if he harms the girl in any way, Chaney will not get his share of the take from their last robbery. However, as soon as Pepper and his gang depart, Chaney decides to kill Mattie in order to silence her. As Chaney prepares to slit Mattie's throat, LaBoeuf strikes him from behind, knocking him unconscious.

Wild West Showdowns

In the valley below, Cogburn faces off against Pepper and three of his accomplices. He kills everyone but Pepper. Cogburn becomes trapped under his horse when the creature is shot. Pepper approaches him with the intention of killing him. But high on the bluff overlooking the valley, LaBoeuf aims his rifle and kills Pepper from afar, a remarkable shot.

But just then, Chaney sneaks up and knocks LaBoeuf out with a rock. He and Mattie grapple for LaBoeuf's rifle. Mattie obtains the rifle, stands up, and shoots Chaney, killing him. However, the kickback from the rifle sends her backward, falling into a pit where she is bitten by a rattlesnake. Together, Cogburn and LaBoeuf pull her out of the pit.

Cogburn races off with Mattie to get her to a doctor, picking her up and running with her when the horse gives out. He makes it to Bagby's store where he collapses with her.

In the final scene, Mattie narrates that 25 years have passed. She reports that when Cogburn arrived at Bagby's store with her, her hand had turned black, necessitating the amputation of her arm. She had been told Cogburn stayed with her until she was out of danger.

Seeking Cogburn

The older Mattie arrives in Memphis, Tennessee, by train, having received a flyer from Cogburn along with a note. Cogburn is now traveling with a Wild West show and invited Mattie to come see him. There, Mattie learns Cogburn passed away three days prior and was buried in the Confederate

The outlaw
Chaney proves
difficult to beat.

cemetery in Jonesboro, Arkansas. She narrates that she had his body moved to her family plot.

Mattie never married and has not seen LaBoeuf since, yet she admits she would be pleased to hear from him. She turns to walk away from Cogburn's grave at the family cemetery. "Time just gets away from us," she reflects.[6]

Mattie proves herself to be as able as the men she travels with.

How to Apply Feminist Criticism to *True Grit*

What Is Feminist Criticism?

Feminist criticism applies the ideas of feminism to a work. Feminism is the belief that women's opportunities and rights should equal those of men's. Historically, most cultures have been patriarchal. Feminist criticism strives to review the film, piece of literature, or other work of art and demonstrate whether common gender stereotypes exist within the work.

Applying Feminist Criticism to *True Grit*

Mattie Ross is the only major female character in *True Grit*. Placed in a situation in which other young girls her age would be stricken with grief, Mattie does not let the death of her father rattle her. Rather, she summons her intelligence, courage, and sense of morality to propel her through her quest to avenge her father's murder. In the Wild West—the classic man's world—Mattie is initially treated as not only a child but also an outsider who has no business in the dealings of men. However, throughout *True Grit*, young Mattie Ross defies female stereotypes, proving herself to be every bit as intelligent and able-bodied as the men who accompany her and gaining their respect.

Mattie is very intelligent, which is evidenced by her knowledge of Latin and mathematics, her ability to verbally spar, and the fact that she is a level-headed businesswoman. When Mattie visits Colonel Stonehill, a man with whom her father had been doing business before his death, Mattie proves her intelligence. Despite his kind remarks, Stonehill makes the mistake of assuming he is dealing with an

Thesis Statement
Here, the author presents her thesis statement: "However, throughout *True Grit,* young Mattie Ross defies female stereotypes, proving herself to be every bit as intelligent and able-bodied as the men who accompany her and gaining their respect." The thesis answers the question of whether Mattie subverts female stereotypes in the film.

Argument One
Here, the author begins her argument about how the film portrays Mattie as an atypical female in film culture: "Mattie is very intelligent, which is evidenced by her knowledge of Latin and mathematics, her ability to verbally spar, and the fact that she is a level-headed businesswoman."

average child. However, Mattie quickly shows she is more quick-witted than the colonel. She dives right into the business of compensation for her father's horse while it was in Stonehill's care. She also forces the man to buy back the ponies he sold her father. After proving to Stonehill her firm grasp on matters ranging from horses, trading, Latin and the law, Stonehill nervously accepts the terms of her agreement. In a nutshell, film reviewer David Thomson correctly defines Mattie as, "intense,

Mattie shows courage even when threatened by dangerous outlaws, including Pepper.

Argument Two
The author continues making her case by expanding her argument: "Despite being repeatedly dismissed by men, Mattie demonstrates conviction, courage, and a strong moral compass throughout the film." This argument shows how Mattie challenges her gender role through her actions.

cunning herself, and more articulate than any 14-year-old of today would dare to be."[1]

Despite being repeatedly dismissed by men, Mattie demonstrates conviction, courage, and a strong moral compass throughout the film. Cogburn, LaBoeuf, Chaney, and numerous others promptly view Mattie as a child and girl. They feel her place is back at home with her mother. However, they all soon come to realize that Mattie can more than hold her own.

Although Cogburn received a taste of Mattie's verbal sparring earlier, he still insists she should return home. He leaves on his quest for Chaney without her.

However, when he sees Mattie boldly cross the river on horseback, Cogburn gets his first glimpse of her ability and bravery. Therefore, Cogburn permits Mattie to accompany him and LaBoeuf. LaBoeuf chooses to treat her as a child and spank her after she insists on following the men on their search, but Cogburn stops him. Cogburn is beginning to realize Mattie does not deserve to be treated like a child.

During the course of the film, Cogburn begins to show more and more respect for Mattie. Cogburn's initial fears that Mattie would be inadequate prove unfounded when he sees Mattie camps like a trooper, rides without tiring, and shows no fear even when faced with outlaws and thieves. Never timid, she doesn't shy away from rebuking Cogburn for his uncouth manners and questionable morals. As Cogburn's doubts begin to fade, he even starts to confide in Mattie a bit of his history, including the story of his divorce, as if she is his peer. Cogburn eventually sees Mattie as an equal on the trail.

By the end of the film, it is evident Cogburn and Mattie each held the other in high regard as they remain in correspondence with one another. Despite him having once viewed Mattie as "a young harpy in trousers," Cogburn's respect for Mattie lasts until his dying day.[2]

As for LaBoeuf, he also begins to see some of Mattie's qualities and grows to see her as an equal. He comes to appreciate

> **Argument Three**
>
> The author sums up the examples in the previous paragraphs, explaining that Cogburn comes to respect Mattie as an equal: "During the course of the film, Cogburn begins to show more and more respect for Mattie."

> **Argument Four**
>
> The author now explores how LaBoeuf's attitude toward Mattie changes: "As for LaBoeuf, he also begins to see some of Mattie's qualities and grows to see her as an equal."

her as a knowledgeable conversationalist, unlike their gruff counterpart. At the dug-out shack, the three discuss Chaney's crimes in Texas, and Mattie proves to be adept with Latin legal phrases, explaining terms LaBoeuf uses to a confused Cogburn. Later, when LaBoeuf parts company with them, Mattie asks him to stay, challenging him to come up with a time when she has held them back. "You've earned your spurs. That is clear enough," he tells her. "You've been a regular old hand on the trail."[3]

> **Conclusion**
> The final paragraph concludes the author's critique and reiterates that Mattie, through her words and actions, has proven to the men she is their equal.

Through Mattie, Cogburn, and LaBoeuf, viewers begin to realize that ability is not dictated by gender. By the time the threesome overcome Chaney and Pepper, Cogburn and LaBoeuf view Mattie as another partner. When Mattie is bitten by a snake, neither man utters a word that she had no business out in the wild. Cogburn simply scoops her up and rides as hard as he can to get her medical attention and then remains by her side. Mattie challenges typical female stereotypes and, in doing so, becomes respected by those around her.

Thinking Critically about *True Grit*

1. Do you agree with the author's thesis? Why or why not? Would you add anything to it? If so, what?

2. How do the villains in the film view Mattie? Do they view her stereotypically? Why or why not?

3. What does the ending say about Mattie's power as a woman? Even though she needs rescuing by Cogburn, the scene does not play out as her being a damsel in distress. How does her behavior as an older woman in the film's final scene reaffirm her strength as a female?

Other Approaches

The critique you have just read is one way to approach *True Grit* through the lens of feminist criticism. Following are two other ways to apply feminist criticism to *True Grit*.

True Grit as Reinforcing Feminist Stereotypes

Although the author took the viewpoint that Mattie subverts classic antifeminist views and is a valuable and capable trail hand, it could be argued that she, in fact, succumbs to the stereotypical trope of damsel in distress by the end of the film. Although she holds her own throughout the journey, in the end, she needs to rely on a male character to save her—twice. Not only does LaBoeuf save her from Chaney, but Cogburn does as well when he rides off with an injured Mattie in his arms.

The thesis statement for such a critique could be: *True Grit* reaffirms the idea that women are reliant upon the protection of men and overstep their boundaries when they enter the world of masculinity.

A New Feminist Role for the Times

In a *Los Angeles Times* article, film critic Rebecca Keegan characterized *True Grit*'s heroine Mattie as follows:

> Given that female adolescents are frequently depicted on-screen as vapid ("Mean Girls"), angst-ridden ("Twilight"), pregnant ("Juno") or merely decorative ("Spider-Man"), Mattie Ross is a remarkable role. She never shakes out her braids in a makeover montage, swoons over a cute stable boy or frets about the daunting task at hand.[4]

The article goes on to quote director Debra Granik as saying, "A young female protagonist doesn't need to have a boyfriend, get pregnant, cut herself or be naked to attract an audience."[5]

In that vein, another way to view Mattie through the lens of feminist criticism is to respond to how Mattie is different from other female film characters.

A possible thesis for this work might be: *True Grit's* Mattie proves female roles in film can be admirable while not succumbing to the archetypes that label women and disempower them.

You Critique It

Now that you have learned about several different critical theories and how to apply them to film, are you ready to perform a critique of your own? You have read that this type of evaluation can help you look at movies from a new perspective and make you pay attention to issues you may not have otherwise recognized. So, why not use one of the critical theories profiled in this book to consider a fresh take on your favorite movie?

First, choose a theory and the movie you want to analyze. Remember that the theory is a springboard for asking questions about the work.

Next, write a specific question that relates to the theory you have selected. Then you can form your thesis, which should provide the answer to that question. Your thesis is the most important part of your critique and offers an argument about the work based on the tenets, or beliefs, of the theory you are applying. Recall that the thesis statement typically appears at the very end of the introductory paragraph of your essay. It is usually only one sentence long.

After you have written your thesis, find evidence to back it up. Good places to start are in the work itself or journals or articles that discuss what other people have said about it. Since you are critiquing a movie, you may also want to read about the director's life to get a sense of what factors may have affected the creative process. This can be useful if working within historical or auteur types of criticism.

Depending on which theory you apply, you can often find evidence in the movie's language, plot, or character development. You should also explore parts of the movie that seem to disprove your thesis and create an argument against them. As you do this, you might want to address what other critics have written about the movie. Their quotes may help support your claim.

Before you start analyzing a work, think about the different arguments made in this book. Reflect on how evidence supporting the thesis was presented. Did you find that some of the techniques used to back up the arguments were more convincing than others? Try these methods as you prove your thesis in your own critique.

When you are finished writing your critique, read it over carefully. Is your thesis statement understandable? Do the supporting arguments flow logically, with the topic of each paragraph clearly stated? Can you add any information that would present your readers with a stronger argument in favor of your thesis? Were you able to use quotes from the movie, as well as from other critics, to enhance your ideas?

Did you see the work in a new light?

Timeline

1954 Joel Coén is born in Saint Louis Park, Minnesota, on November 29.

1957 Ethan Coen is born in Saint Louis Park on September 21.

1984 Joel and actress Frances McDormand wed on April 1; *Blood Simple* is released.

1987 The Coens' *Raising Arizona* hits the big screen.

1990 Mobster flick *Miller's Crossing* is released to favorable reviews.

1991 *Barton Fink* is released and wins Best Picture at the Cannes Film Festival.

1994 *The Hudsucker Proxy* is released but is not as successful as the Coens' previous films.

1996 The Coens' dark comedy *Fargo* is released, garnering critical acclaim and earning Joel an award for Best Director at the Cannes Film Festival.

1997 *Fargo* receives seven Academy Award nominations. The brothers take home an Oscar for Best Screenplay. McDormand receives the Oscar for Best Actress.

1998 The Coens continue to exemplify creative filmmaking with the release of *The Big Lewbowski.*

1971 Joel enters Simon's Rock
in Great Barrington, Massachusetts.

1973 Upon graduating from Simon's Rock, Joel
enters the New York University film program.

1974 Ethan enrolls in Simon's Rock.

1977 Ethan begins studies at Princeton University
as a philosophy major.

1980 Upon graduation, Ethan moves to
New York and joins his brother working
as a production assistant. The brothers
begin writing *Blood Simple*.

1982 Joel and Ethan shoot their
first film, *Blood Simple*.

2000 *O Brother, Where Art Thou?* is released.
The film receives glowing reviews and two
Academy Award nominations.

2001 *The Man Who Wasn't There* is released
and earns Joel a Best Director award
at the Cannes Film Festival.

2003 *Intolerable Cruelty*, starring George
Clooney and Catherine Zeta-Jones,
is released.

2007 *No Country for Old Men* hits the big screen. Critics
praise the film and it receives two Golden Globes
and four Academy Awards.

2009 *A Serious Man* debuts at the box office.

2010 *True Grit*, starring Jeff Bridges,
Matt Damon, and Hailee Steinfeld,
becomes a box office hit. The film
receives ten Academy Award
nominations.

Glossary

archetype

    A recurring plot, character, or theme in literature.

brain trust

    A group of advisers.

collective unconscious

    According to Carl Jung, a part of a person's
unconscious mind that is common to all people.

constituency

    A body of citizens who are able to vote.

harpy

    A bad-tempered woman.

nihilist

    A person who adheres to the beliefs of nihilism,
a viewpoint that rejects values and beliefs, and
deems social organization, laws, and institutions as
pointless.

pacifism

    Opposition to war or violence of any kind.

pardon

An official release from the penalties of one's crime.

paterfamilias

The male head of a household.

patriarchal

Of or relating to the father.

social norm

Behavioral expectations within a society or group.

stereotype

A traditional concept or type.

subvert

To undermine authority.

trope

A common theme or device.

White Russian

An alcoholic mixed drink consisting of vodka, coffee liqueur, and cream or milk.

Bibliography of Works and Criticism

Important Works

Blood Simple, 1984

Raising Arizona, 1987

Miller's Crossing, 1990

Barton Fink, 1991

The Hudsucker Proxy, 1994

Fargo, 1996

The Big Lebowski, 1998

O Brother, Where Art Thou?, 2000

The Man Who Wasn't There, 2001

Intolerable Cruelty, 2003

The Ladykillers, 2004

No Country for Old Men, 2007

A Serious Man, 2009

True Grit, 2010

Critical Discussions

Braudy, Leo, and Marshall Cohen, eds. *Film Theory and Criticism: Introductory Readings*. New York: Oxford UP, 2009. Print

Conard, Mark T., ed. *The Philosophy of The Coen Brothers*. Lexington, KY: The UP of Kentucky, 2009. Print.

Doom, Ryan P. *The Brothers Coen: Unique Characters of Violence*. Santa Barbara, CA: ABC-CLIO, 2009. Print.

Woods, Paul A., ed. *Joel and Ethan Coen: Blood Siblings*. London: Plexus, 2003. Print.

Resources

Selected Bibliography

The Big Lebowski. Dir. Joel Coen. Twentieth Century Fox, 1998. Film.

Fargo. Dir. Joel Coen. Twentieth Century Fox, 1996. Film.

O Brother, Where Art Thou? Dir. Joel Coen. Twentieth Century Fox, 2000. Film.

Palmer, R. Barton. *Joel and Ethan Coen*. Chicago: U of Illinois P, 2004. Print.

Robson, Eddie. *Coen Brothers*. London: Virgin Films, 2003. Print.

True Grit. Dir. Joel Coen and Ethan Coen. Paramount Pictures Corporation, 2010. Film.

Further Readings

Bergen, Ronald. *The Coen Brothers*. New York: Thunder's Mouth, 2000. Print.

Falsani, Cathleen. *The Dude Abides: the Gospel According to the Coen Brothers*. Grand Rapids, MI: Zondervan, 2009. Print.

Rowell, Erica. *The Brothers Grim: the Films of Ethan and Joel Coen*. Lanham, MD: The Scarecrow, 2007. Print.

Web Links

To learn more about critiquing the films of the Coen brothers, visit ABDO Publishing Company online at **www.abdopublishing.com**. Web sites about the films of the Coen brothers are featured on our Book Links page. These links are routinely monitored and updated to provide the most current information available.

For More Information

The Academy of Motion Picture Arts and Sciences

8949 Wilshire Boulevard, Beverly Hills, CA 990211

310-247-3000

www.oscars.org

Read about the history of the Academy Awards and past winners.

San Francisco Film Museum

1755 Van Ness Avenue, Suite 101, San Francisco, CA 94109

415-652-0249

sanfranciscofilmmuseum.org

The San Francisco Film Museum examines the history of filmmaking.

Source Notes

Chapter 1. Introduction to Critiques

None.

Chapter 2. A Closer Look at the Coen Brothers

None.

Chapter 3. An Overview of *O Brother, Where Art Thou?*

    1. *O Brother, Where Art Thou?*. Dir. Joel Coen.
Touchstone Pictures, 2000. Film.

    2. Ibid.

    3. Ibid.

    4. Ibid.

Chapter 4. How to Apply New Criticism to *O Brother, Where Art Thou?*

    1. *O Brother, Where Art Thou?*. Dir. Joel Coen.
Touchstone Pictures, 2000. Film.

    2. Ibid.

    3. Ibid.

    4. Ibid.

Chapter 5. An Overview of *Fargo*

    1. *Fargo*. Dir. Joel Coen. MGM Home
Entertainment, 1996. Film.

Chapter 6. How to Apply Gender Criticism to *Fargo*

1. *Fargo*. Dir. Joel Coen. MGM Home Entertainment, 1996. Film.

2. Ibid.

Chapter 7. An Overview of *The Big Lebowski*

1. *The Big Lebowski*. Dir. Joel Coen. Polygram Filmed Entertainment, 1998. Film.

2. Ibid.

3. Ibid.

Chapter 8. How to Apply Archetypal Criticism to *The Big Lebowski*

1. *The Big Lebowski*. Dir. Joel Coen. Polygram Filmed Entertainment, 1998. Film.

2. Ibid.

3. Ibid.

4. William J. Hynes. "Mapping the Characteristics of Mythic Tricksters: A Heuristic Guide." *Mythical Trickster Figures: Contours, Contexts, and Criticisms*. Tuscaloosa, AL: U of Alabama P. 1993. Print. 33-45.

5. *The Big Lebowski*. Dir. Joel Coen. Polygram Filmed Entertainment, 1998. Film.

6. Ibid.

7. Ibid.

8. Ibid.

Source Notes Continued

Chapter 9. An Overview of *True Grit*

1. *True Grit*. Dir. Joel Coen and Ethan Coen. Paramount Pictures Corporation, 2010. Film.

2. Ibid.

3. Ibid.

4. Ibid.

5. Ibid.

6. Ibid.

Chapter 10. How to Apply Feminist Criticism to *True Grit*

1. *True Grit*. Dir. Joel Coen and Ethan Coen. Paramount Pictures Corporation, 2010. Film.

2. Ibid.

3. Ibid.

4. Rebecca Keegan. "Teen girls in film showcase true grit." *LA Times Online*. 9 Jan. 2011. Web. 23 Jan. 2012.

5. Ibid.

Index

Essential Critiques

About the Author

Susan E. Hamen is a full-time editor and freelance writer who finds her most rewarding career experiences to be writing children's books. She has written books on various historical topics, including the Wright brothers, the Industrial Revolution and the New Deal. Her book *Clara Barton: Civil War Hero and American Red Cross Founder* was chosen for the ALA's 2011 Amelia Bloomer Project Book List. This is Hamen's twelfth book. She lives in Minnesota with her husband and two children.

Photo Credits

Pascal Le Segretain/Getty Images, cover, 3; Laurent Rebours/ AP Images, 12; Steve Granitz/WireImage/Getty Images, 19, 98; Buena Vista Pictures/Everett Collection, 20, 33, 35; Buena Vista Pictures/Photofest, 23, 27, 30; Gramercy Pictures/ Photofest, 40, 43, 48; Gramercy Pictures/Everett Collection, 53, 63, 66, 73; Everett Collection, 58; Paramount Pictures/ Photofest, 78, 86, 99; Lorey Sebastian/Paramount Pictures/ Photofest, 81, 85, 89